A Bible Study from

GREG LAURIE

BASED ON THE FEATURE FILM

BEN-HUR

FIGHT THE GOOD FIGHT. FINISH THE RACE.

AS DEVELOPED WITH
NIC ALLEN

Published by B&H Publishing Group®

Greg Laurie ©2016

BEN-HUR ©2016 Metro-Goldwyn-Mayer Pictures Inc. and Paramount Pictures Corporation. All Rights Reserved.

METRO-GOLDWYN-MAYER is a trademark of Metro-Goldwyn-Mayer Lion Corp. © 2016 Metro-Goldwyn-Mayer Studios Inc. All Rights Reserved.

ISBN: 978-1-4300-6798-6

Item: 005792810

Dewey decimal classification Number: 233.7

Subject heading: FAITH \ GOD--WILL \ CHOICE (PSYCHOLOGY)

Printed in the United States of America.

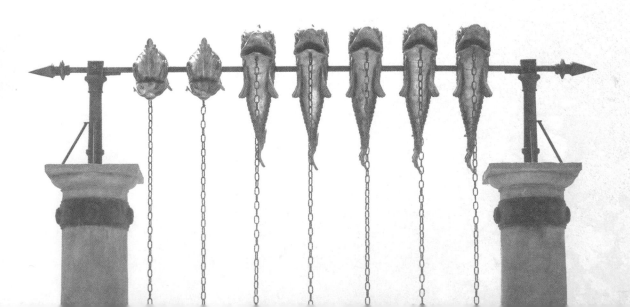

TABLE OF CONTENTS

ABOUT THE AUTHORS

GREG LAURIE

Greg Laurie, senior pastor of Harvest Christian Fellowship® in Riverside and Irvine, California, began his pastoral ministry at age 19 by leading a Bible study of 30 people. Since then, God has transformed that small group into a church of some 15,000 people, making Harvest one of the largest churches in America. In 1990, Laurie began holding large-scale public evangelistic events called Harvest Crusades®. Since that time, more than 5.2 million people have attended Harvest Crusades across the United States. Greg and his wife, Cathe, have two sons, Christopher and Jonathan. Christopher went to be with the Lord in 2008. They also have five grandchildren.

NIC ALLEN

Nic currently serves as the Discipleship Pastor at Rolling Hills Community Church in Franklin, TN where he has lead in various pastoral roles for nine years. Nic and his wife Susan married in 2000. While they are incredibly passionate about seeing people come alive in Christ through the study of God's word, their primary disciple-making role these days is for their three young children: Lillie Cate, Nora Blake, and Simon.

ABOUT THE MOVIE

BEN-HUR

FIGHT THE GOOD FIGHT. FINISH THE RACE.

Ben-Hur is a major Paramount Pictures/MGM motion picture bursting with action—including a new chariot race for the ages—and elevated by Christian themes of justice, liberty, redemption, and radical forgiveness. It tells the classic story of Judah Ben–Hur (Jack Huston), a prince falsely accused of treason by his adopted brother Messala (Toby Kebbell), an officer in the Roman army. Stripped of his title and separated from his family and the woman he loves (Nazanin Boniadi), Judah is forced into slavery and despair.

After years at sea, a breathtaking turn of events sends Judah on an epic journey back to his homeland to seek revenge, where chance encounters with Jesus of Nazareth (Rodrigo Santoro) transform his life and lead him to discover grace, mercy, and ultimately, redemption. Based on Lew Wallace's timeless novel, *Ben-Hur: A Tale of the Christ.* Also starring Morgan Freeman in an unforgettable performance.

The film stars Jack Huston, Toby Kebbell, Rodrigo Santoro, Nazanin Boniadi, Ayelet Zurer, and Morgan Freeman.

INTRODUCTION

FIGHT THE GOOD FIGHT. FINISH THE RACE.

Although set in Ancient Rome, Ben-Hur's story could easily be yours. You may never face unjust arrest or life as a slave, but you are no doubt faced with choices that will inevitably lead to sacrifice. Even after trusting Christ as Lord, we must continually submit to Him and choose His way over our own agenda.

You may not be the Ben-Hur of your day, but this Bible study is a chance to encounter Christ in a new, fresh way. The next five weeks will allow you to explore who Jesus is, what He did, and why it matters today. This study serves as an opportunity to walk in the time of Christ and to understand, deepen, and share your faith in Him.

For the early Christians, believing in Christ was difficult, but they had the advantage of a face-to-face encounter with Jesus. Two thousand years later, we don't have that same advantage. Trusting Christ, whom we have never physically seen or touched, can be hard. Our faith can easily falter at times. This study is an opportunity for you to "see" the person of Jesus in a way you've never seen Him before through the eyes of various New Testament characters.

Through this Bible study, you will be invited to seek the Kingdom of God, practice compassion, identify in Christ's suffering on the cross, tell someone the powerful story of God's grace, and extend to others the forgiveness Christ has given you. This study will remind you that faith is not only a one-time event but also a lifelong journey of trust and commitment to Jesus Christ.

HOW TO USE THIS STUDY

The Ben-Hur Bible Study contains five lessons to use for group or personal Bible study. Each lesson contains four elements: Introduction, Teaching Video Discussion, Engage Lesson, and then Devotional Homework consisting of three days of personal study. Allow 45 to 60 minutes for each group session.

1. **INTRODUCTION:** Each study begins with an introductory overview of the coming lesson. This section is designed for use in a group setting, but it can also be adapted for personal study. If you are in a group, read through the section and answer the introductory questions together.

2. **TEACHING VIDEO DISCUSSION:** The Bible study DVD features teaching videos from pastor and author Greg Laurie to accompany each session. In each video, Pastor Laurie will discuss a specific scene from the movie and the gospel implications of that scene. Each video is 4-5 minutes long and features discussion questions based on the teaching points.

3. **ENGAGE LESSON:** This section is the primary focus of each week. Leaders should spend the majority of the group time teaching while using verses and questions in this section to guide discussion.

4. **DEVOTIONAL HOMEWORK:** Lastly, leaders should assign class members the three days of personal Bible study to complete at home before the next group session. Through this, members of your group will be able to dive deeper into the lesson concepts and life application.

A LETTER TO LEADERS

Judah Ben-Hur had a choice to make. He could choose to pursue his own agenda of personal gain and revenge, or he could choose to trust Christ and follow in the ways of God. You decided to take time out of your normal weekly routine to lead others through this small-group Bible study experience. This choice required at least some sacrifice on your part. Thank you for being obedient to the call to lead.

Our prayer is that God will use and guide you as you lead others through the story of Judah Ben-Hur, which ultimately points to the story of Jesus Christ. Along the way, you will engage with many characters from Scripture. We pray you will lead your group to find their own story of redemption in the pages of this study.

This study can play a significant role in the lives of believers and nonbelievers. Historical fiction provides a lens to see the world of Jesus Christ come alive before our eyes. Your group will have the opportunity to walk with characters from Scripture in a way they may have never imagined.

To make the most of this study, we encourage everyone in your group to see the film prior to week one. The movie provides the context for the study. If possible, see the movie as a group before beginning the weekly Bible study.

Make the weekly group gathering a priority. A key theme throughout this study is relationships and the beauty of Christ bringing people together from all different walks of life. Use your group time each week to foster spiritual growth as group members challenge one another in their faith journeys.

Whether this is your tenth time leading a Bible study or your first, you may be experiencing some fear about leading this study. Don't worry! You're not leading this study because you're perfect or because you have everything figured out. Just as you'll see throughout this Bible study, God calls imperfect people to accomplish His will in the world. And like those He called before you, God will equip you to do His work. We pray that as you guide others through this study you'll see God working in your life and sense the Holy Spirit carrying you.

The best way for you to prepare each week is to complete the study yourself. Allow God to prune you in your personal time with Him. Be open and transparent with your group, revealing areas where God is working in you. Pray that God will direct your conversations each week and empower you to lead well. We believe He will! Thank you for being a faithful servant and leading others in this way.

BEN-HUR
Session One

ENCOUNTER WITH A CARPENTER AND HIS KINGDOM

Judah Ben-Hur is an affluent Jewish prince caught in the middle of loyalty to his people, sympathy for the Zealots, and his personal relationship with Rome through his childhood friend Messala. In a simple carpenter's shop he unknowingly encounters the Messiah, and his life will never be the same.

"What is this wisdom given to Him, and how are these miracles performed by His hands? Isn't this the carpenter, the son of Mary, and the brother of James, Joses, Judas, and Simon?" (Mark 6:2-3)

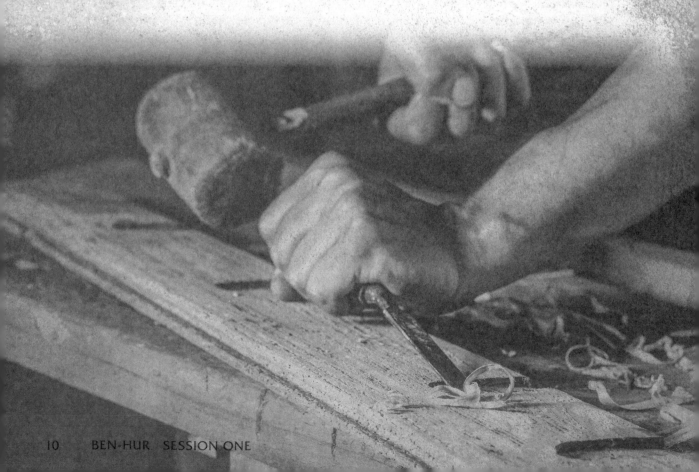

GATHER

Welcome to week one. If you've already seen the movie, you know that it follows the adventure of fictional character Judah Ben-Hur. When we meet Ben-Hur, he is plagued with anger, bitterness, and thoughts of revenge—until he encounters Jesus. If you are a follower of Christ, you know that Jesus changes everything.

During his first meeting with the Messiah, Judah-Ben Hur hears the following statements from Jesus:

> *"Freedom will be found elsewhere."* (see Luke 4:18)

> *"Love your enemies."* (Matt. 5:44)

> *"My kingdom is not of this world."* (John 18:36)

Which of Jesus' statements most entices you to seek a better understanding of Christ?

What about Christ's Kingdom makes you want to know Jesus more?

This week is all about encountering Jesus, the man with a mission. As we begin, be honest about where you are currently in your relationship with God. Where would you place yourself on the scale below?

- ☐ I am a long-time, committed follower of Christ seeking to deepen my faith and intimacy with Jesus.

- ☐ I am a fairly new believer in Jesus seeking to grow in my faith and daily walk with Him.

- ☐ I am exploring Christianity and the claims of Jesus, trying to determine His place in my life.

- ☐ I am indifferent to the message of Christ, but am open to learning how the film connects with the Bible.

If you feel comfortable, share briefly with the group which statement you chose and why. There are no right or wrong answers.

What are your hopes for this study? Are you ready to experience a real, genuine encounter with the person of Jesus Christ? Are you open to the changes His presence might bring about in your life? Are you willing to let other believers challenge you?

If you said yes, then get ready—because Jesus changes everything.

WATCH

As a group, view the week one teaching video with Greg Laurie. Read the summary below before watching the video. Then discuss the teaching video together using the questions provided.

Summary:

In this teaching segment, Greg Laurie highlights the first moment that Judah Ben-Hur meets Jesus in the carpentry shop. We know very little about the life of Jesus between His childhood (see Luke 2:41-52) and the moment His public ministry began (see Luke 3:23). Tradition tells us Jesus was a carpenter. In the film, Jesus offers Judah profound words about the Messiah and God's plan to give peace. Greg Laurie explains the difference between the Messiah people expected and the Messiah God sent, as well as the kingdom rule of Roman oppression versus the coming rule of Christ's true Kingdom.

Discuss:

1. *What was life like for Jews like Judah Ben-Hur during the climate of Roman occupation in Israel?*

2. *According to Laurie, Zealots rose in opposition to harsh Roman rule. How do you think you would have responded in similar circumstances? How do you respond when you feel you have been treated unfairly?*

3. *According to the teaching video, what is the only way to change a human heart? Share the story of how Jesus has changed you since you invited Him into your heart.*

4. *Even though we aren't under Roman oppression today, how are followers of Jesus called to live in light of the difficulties we face? How are Christians called to live as part of Christ's coming Kingdom?*

ENGAGE

Read Jesus' words from Matthew 6:25-34.

> *What command does Jesus repeat throughout this passage?*

The people listening to Jesus' teaching were no strangers to physical need. The socio-economic climate was one of intense poverty and the constant struggle to meet basic needs. Jesus preached a message of hope-filled endurance.

> *What are some everyday life concerns facing your group?*

> *How does building up our earthly kingdoms give us cause for anxiety?*

The difficulties we face can result in two opposite responses. Anxieties can either cause us to doubt God or turn to Him in faith and develop greater maturity in our view of His sovereignty.

> *In what ways do your difficulties cause you to doubt Jesus or seek Him?*

> *What does it look like for you to tangibly seek God's kingdom and His righteousness?*

The Jews under Roman rule had high hopes for the promised Messiah. When Jesus arrived on the scene, they expected Him to overthrow Rome and bring God's people safety and security. But He did not come to establish an earthly Kingdom. Yet.

> *Where do people in the world today look for hope and salvation? What are some common misconceptions regarding who or what can set things right?*

Judah Ben-Hur assumed that vengeance and restoration of his earthly family would satisfy his greatest need in life. Instead, through Jesus, Judah discovered a different way. Christ will return one day and establish His eternal rule as King. In the meantime, living as part of that kingdom means seeking the rule and reign of Christ in every area of life, knowing that true peace and total freedom come from Him alone.

> *What areas of your life do you need to stop trying to control and hand over to God instead?*

Pray now and ask God to establish His rule in your life every day and in every area. Ask Him to give you the peace and freedom that only comes from Him.

INDIVIDUAL STUDY: DAY ONE

This week is about submitting to the rule and reign of Jesus in every area of our lives. And Jesus has given us power through the Holy Spirit to help us carry out this task.

In the book of Acts, Luke records Christ's final words to His followers before He ascended to heaven. Even after all Jesus' disciples had seen and experienced, they still hoped He would restore the physical kingdom of Israel. Read Acts 1:7-8 to see Jesus' response.

> **He said to them, "It is not for you to know times or periods that the Father has set by His own authority. But you will receive power when the Holy Spirit has come on you, and you will be My witnesses in Jerusalem, in all Judea and Samaria, and to the ends of the earth."**

Jesus issued power to His disciples but not the kind they expected. Underline the word "witnesses" above. In Greek, it's the word *martus,* which means that followers of Jesus, because of the endowment of the Holy Spirit, will be witnesses of the salvation of Jesus.[1] It's also the word used to describe Stephen, the first Christian martyr in Acts 22:20, and the Greek term on which we base our understanding of martyrdom.[2]

How were the early believers witnesses of Jesus?

Consider someone you know who is deeply focused on God's kingdom, constantly pursuing and exemplifying the righteousness of Christ. In your opinion, what makes this person's life seem unique?

Think of a time in your own life when you have been a witness for Jesus. How did the Holy Spirit help you?

A true encounter with Jesus Christ changes a person. The Bible teaches that Godly sorrow brings repentance that leads to salvation (2 Cor. 7:10). Something happens when when people recognize their sin and respond to God in repentance. That act is characterized by:

- confessing your sinful condition before God

- expressing your desire to be forgiven by God

- walking away from sin with the power of God

Throughout this study, you'll engage with various New Testament characters. Each encountered Jesus differently. In each of their stories, you'll discover a piece of your own story and be able to link their experience with Jesus to your own repentance and ultimately to your call as a witness of the risen Christ.

To ready yourself for the task ahead, answer the following questions about your initial encounters with Jesus.

When were you introduced to faith in Jesus? Describe the circumstances surrounding your life at the time.

Who shaped your earliest understanding of who Jesus was and what He did?

If you are not yet a believer, what questions or reservations do you have concerning Christianity?

If you feel inadequate as a witness for Christ, remember He has given you power through the Holy Spirit. Thank God for the presence of His Spirit in your life, and ask Him to give you boldness to witness to the world.

INDIVIDUAL STUDY: DAY TWO

Ben-Hur may have been a prince at the start of the film, but we know he did not remain one. Much of the plot revolves around his time as a slave seeking the restoration of his family and revenge on Messala.

Jesus Christ was born to laboring peasants and, like other Jewish boys, adopted the trade of His father. Read Mark 6:1-3 and note what can be determined about Jesus' background and experience as a minister in His hometown.

Jesus' hometown:

Jesus' profession:

Jesus' family members:

The Greek word for carpenter is *tekton* and it means "wood worker."[3] Jesus could have crafted homes or furnishings. Perhaps He repaired and refinished. Some scholars assert that *tekton* can also be interpreted as stone-masonry. Jesus' trade could have been far broader than our limited interpretations allow.[4] Regardless of the specific details of Jesus' job, the incarnate God-man didn't come as a prince or ruler but a common laborer. That detail matters.

Describe the reaction of the crowds upon Jesus' return to His hometown. Why do you think it was difficult for them to believe Jesus' words?

Judging from the local reaction, you may have guessed that the gospel-centric encounter with Jesus we are exploring today is that of the unbeliever.

Imagine living in Nazareth.

Knowing the local carpenter Joseph and his boys.

Seeing them play in the streets.

Watching them grow up.

Buying their hand-crafted goods and services.

Now hearing stories about Jesus' travels.

The rumors about His abilities.

The talk of His teaching.

Imagine Jesus coming home. Would you be able to accept everything that seemed to have changed about Jesus, or would memories of the young carpenter be too odd to overcome?

Now consider Judah Ben-Hur and all the times his character in the film must have called on local tradesmen, including carpenters. Skilled laborers would not have typically been associated with religious philosophy or scholarship. Yet from Jesus the carpenter Ben-Hur heard about freedom, forgiveness, and a kingdom yet to come.

Read the following passages regarding encounters people had with Jesus. Note why each chose not to believe.

Mark 10:17-27:

Matthew 9:32-34:

John 10:31-39:

In each of these passages, including the Nazarenes in Mark 6, people encountered Jesus but could not overcome a specific hurdle that prevented their belief. Whether it was law and tradition, history and familiarity, or fear and resentment, something kept them from seeing who Jesus really was.

In your earliest encounters with Jesus, what were the specific barriers to your belief?

Do any of those still exist?

Read John 10:37-38 again. The works Jesus did supported His claim to be the Son of God.

What work has Jesus done in your life that helped you overcome your barriers to belief?

What Scriptures can you reflect on that assert Jesus' work?

Judah Ben-Hur would one day see Jesus' words to him about freedom and forgiveness come true. Christ's work on the cross would more than validate His claim to be the Son of God. It accomplished all He came to do for us, overcame every obstacle, and provided all the proof we could ever need.

Ask God to identify barriers to your belief and open your eyes to the work of Jesus that can overcome those barriers.

INDIVIDUAL STUDY: DAY THREE

To the Pharisees of Jesus' day, God's will was confined to a system of laws. Power was the religious authority they lorded over others.

To the Zealot, God's will was confined to a political kingdom that must be established. Power equaled the might of a movement large enough to overthrow the Roman regime.

To the Jewish tax collector, God's will was trumped by opportunism. Power meant alignment with Rome even if it meant exploiting one's own people.

Jesus didn't just call and save those who could easily adapt to His Kingdom ways. He called outliers and enemies to be His disciples.

Read Matthew 9:9-13.

> **Who encountered Jesus in this passage?**

> **What was his profession or status in life?**

> **What was his response to Jesus' invitation?**

Tax collectors were the most hated men in the community. Because of their alignment with Rome basically to rob their fellow Jews, tax collectors were not permitted to attend synagogue or participate in worship. Religiously, the Jewish community regarded them as worse off than a Gentile.[5]

Read John 3:1-21 and John 19:38-42.

> **Who encountered Jesus in John 3?**

> **What was his profession or status in life?**

> **Based on John 19, how did this person ultimately respond to Jesus?**

In general, the Pharisees and religious leaders were violently opposed to Jesus, although some came to believe in Him. For those who did, it benefited them to keep it secret because of the societal pressures surrounding Jesus at the time. Joseph of Arimathea was such a leader. As a member of the Sanhedrin, the religious council that convicted Jesus, it's easy to see why he kept his faith under wraps. The same could be said of Nicodemus.

> *Have you ever felt pressured to keep silent about your belief in Jesus? How so?*

Read Luke 6:15.

It's easy to gloss over verses like this one, but the Bible's details are intentional. There are no other specific details given about this second Simon, but his status as a Zealot is an important one. It meant that he would have fought violently against the Romans and directly opposed anyone who welcomed them or benefited from their presence, namely the tax collectors.

That Jesus called both Matthew the tax collector and Simon the Zealot reminds us just how much a sinner changes when under the kingdom rule and reign of Jesus in their hearts.

Close today's study by reading John 6:66-69.

> *What does this passage say about how many of Jesus' followers responded to the difficulties of following Him?*

Matthew the tax collector and Simon the Zealot were among the twelve who remained. They are included again in Acts 1 with those who were present at Jesus' ascension. Through it all, many people very far from Christ's kingdom became His closest followers and went on to launch the church and change the world. Scripture paints a continual portrait for us of people far from God who were powerfully transformed by Jesus.

Compose a prayer of thankfulness for His invitation of salvation. Thank Him for His work in your life to bring you near to Him. Ask God to draw you even closer to Him in the coming weeks.

BEN-HUR
Session Two

ENCOUNTER WITH A CHRIST WHO UNDERSTANDS

The carpenter who once shared wisdom with Judah Ben-Hur enters for a second encounter—this time to offer a hand of compassion in the form of a refreshing cup of water. Jesus, our Savior and Lord, served a hurting, betrayed man in his time of greatest need.

"Moved with compassion, Jesus reached out . . . " (Mark 1:41)

GATHER

Welcome to week two. Begin this week by sharing portions of your individual study experience from week one.

> **What stood out most to you during last week's group discussion or personal Bible study?**

> **In what ways were you challenged to live for God's Kingdom instead of building an earthly kingdom?**

> **Last week in Matthew 9, you read the account of Jesus calling Matthew the tax collector as His disciple. What was the general perception of tax collectors in Jesus' day?**

Scripture gives us numerous other redemptive stories of tax collectors:

- Jesus' parable of the humble tax collector (Luke 18:9-14)
- Jesus visits Zacchaeus the tax collector (Luke 19:1-10)
- Jesus dines with sinners and tax collectors (Luke 15:1-2)

> **Based on these accounts, how did Jesus display compassion toward the tax collectors?**

> **Why is the inclusion of tax collectors in each of these stories so significant?**

Jesus didn't just eat with sinners. He ate with sinners and tax collectors. Jesus didn't compare and contrast the prayer of a Pharisee and an adulterer. He compared a Pharisee and a tax collector. If there is redemption for those considered the worst of sinners, then it must be real for everyone else too. Showing compassion to someone who is habitually tardy and doesn't respect another person's time is one thing. Showing mercy to a convicted murderer is altogether different—at least humanly speaking.

If Christ could forgive society's worst, His love must be significant. As you encounter the compassion of Christ in this week's study, keep the image of the tax collector at the front of your mind.

> **Since Jesus showed compassion to the worst of the worst, how does that help us to experience compassion from Him and share it with others?**

WATCH

As a group, view the week two teaching video with Greg Laurie. Read the summary below before watching the video. Then discuss the teaching video together using the questions provided.

Summary:

In this segment, Greg Laurie unpacks the scene from the film where a convicted Judah Ben-Hur is now experiencing the worst of Roman cruelty after taking the blame for a crime he didn't commit. Jesus spots Ben-Hur in a moment of immense difficulty and offers Him incredible compassion. The same authority who controls the universe also shows us kindness in our suffering. It comes in Christ's presence because He will never leave us. It also comes as Christ's purpose because it accomplishes His greater good in our lives.

Discuss:

1. *Jesus could have easily rescued Judah from imprisonment, but simply provided a cold drink instead. Has God ever responded to your needs in a way you didn't quite expect? Why do you think He works in this way?*

2. *According to the video, what is one reason suffering exists in our lives?*

3. *Tell the group about a time when you experienced a tangible display of Christ's compassion when you needed it most.*

ENGAGE

As a group, compose a definition of the word *compassion*, and write it below.

Compassion is:

Baker's Evangelical Dictionary of Theology defines compassion as: *That [human] disposition that fuels acts of kindness and mercy.*[1]

In the New Testament Greek, *compassion* is a form of the word *splagchnizomai* and literally means "to be moved in ones bowels" because the gut was thought to be the source of love and pity.[2] In addition to *compassion*, it's often translated as "to love, to pity, and to show mercy." Compassion is connected to action.

Beside each passage below, identify the people Christ showed compassion to and why you think Jesus was moved to act on behalf of each group.

> Matthew 9:35-38:
>
> Matthew 14:13-14:
>
> Matthew 20:29-34:
>
> *Compare the needs of these biblical characters with the needs of those in your community today. Have you seen God show this same type of compassion to those you know who have similar needs?*

Jesus' compassion is a repeated theme throughout the gospels. Of course there is no greater act of mercy or compassion than willingly dying in someone else's place. John 15:13 says, "No one has greater love than this, that someone would lay down his life for his friends." Jesus' ultimate act of compassion toward us was His sacrifice on the cross. The great love He showed in His death extends mercy to us even in our darkest hours.

> *What does it mean to you that Jesus calls us "friends?"*

Read John 4:14. Considering these words from Jesus, discuss the symbolism of the cup of water Jesus gave Judah Ben-Hur in the film.

> *Although Jesus did not free Ben-Hur from his physical imprisonment, what did Christ ultimately offer him instead?*

Close in prayer today and ask God to refresh your group through your personal studies this week. Thank Him for the love and compassion He shows His people. Thank Him for the ways He has shown us mercy for our earthly trials and for His ultimate act of compassion on the cross that gave us the gift of eternal life.

INDIVIDUAL STUDY: DAY ONE

Read Luke 7:11-17, and answer the following questions.

Who encountered Jesus in this passage?

What were her circumstances, and why did she need compassion?

What miracle did Jesus provide?

Widows are a common theme throughout Scripture. Read the following verses, and make a note of what each has to say about widows.

Deuteronomy 27:19:

Isaiah 1:17:

Exodus 22:22:

1 Timothy 5:3:

James 1:27:

The plight of widows in the ancient world was particularly distressing. Honorable employment for women barely existed. Without fathers, husbands, brothers, or sons to care for them, widows often lived as poverty-stricken outcasts. In the Roman world, no government or social provisions existed for Jews, so widows found themselves without hope.[3] In Luke 7:12, not only did this woman lose a child she loved, but without any caretakers left, her hopes for the future were at stake. The resurrection of her son restored her hope.

We don't have the privilege of knowing how the woman responded to Jesus' miracle. In the space below, write words or phrases you think might describe her reaction.

In this instance, Christ's compassion resulted in a reversal of a physical problem. The widow received her son back. A high view of God's sovereignty and even a basic understanding of His unlimited power means believing that He remains capable to perform miracles like that even today. There are moments when He chooses to remove troubles. There are also moments when God chooses not to remove them but to compassionately provide strength, care, and wisdom to help us walk through the difficulties. Both express His compassion.

Write down a time in your life when God's compassion toward you removed trouble or reversed negative circumstances.

It's not wrong to ask God to remove difficulty in our lives. Paul did it (2 Cor. 12:8), and so did Jesus (Luke 22:42). But we can't expect God to remove difficulty every time. As believers, we know we will share in Christ's sufferings, but we know He will also provide comfort (2 Cor. 1:5).

Write down a time in your life when God's compassion toward you helped you navigate a difficult time.

In what ways did you sense Christ's compassion during that season?

How was God glorified in your suffering?

In contrast to the widow, Christ did not release Judah Ben-Hur from his state of suffering, but He still showed him compassion. Even in our trials and difficulties, God is working according to His gracious will.

Read the following verses, and write how each passage instructs us to respond when we don't see an immediate solution to our trials.

Romans 8:28:

James 1:2-3:

Do you know someone who needs encouragement today? While you may not have the power to raise a loved one from the dead, you can follow Christ's example and act with tenderness.

In the space below, write down all the tangible ways you can show kindness to someone this week.

Beyond meeting physical needs, how can you show Christ's love to people in their difficulties?

Close your time today in prayer, expressing gratitude to God for both the times when He has removed troubles in your life and the times when His great compassion has sustained you through them. Ask God to open your eyes to the needs of those around you.

INDIVIDUAL STUDY: DAY TWO

Begin this session with a personal assessment. Complete the following statements by filling in the blanks with the first response that comes to mind.

- Today I feel very _____ in my walk with Christ.

- This Bible study experience for me so far can best be described as _____.

- My top personal prayer concern in this moment is _____.

- I sense Christ's compassion currently in _____.

- _____ is someone to whom I need to increase my level of compassion.

In today's personal study, you'll explore ways you can receive and model Christ's compassion in your own life.

Self-examination can be very difficult, partly because we don't always like the pictures we see of ourselves when we're honest. Start by identifying the qualities about yourself that you feel are lovely or lovable.

Now, list parts of your identity where you need the grace of Christ.

Scripture is clear that all men are sinful (see Rom. 3:10,23). Nothing about us is worthy of God's love. Although Judah Ben-Hur was innocent of the crime for which he was charged, no man is innocent before God. Christ's compassion toward Ben-Hur in the film is a beautiful portrait of Christ's compassion toward all suffering. The true act of compassion is that of a loving Savior who extends mercy despite the fact that it is undeserved.

Read Matthew 15:32-39.

To whom did Christ extend compassion in this passage?

What concern did Jesus have for the people's well-being of the people in this instance?

Jesus' act to the crowd was similar to what you saw in the film. Jesus gave the crowds food because they were hungry. He gave Judah Ben-Hur water to relieve his thirst. But Ben-Hur's refreshing gift of water from Jesus would not have been enough to physically sustain him for the cruel days ahead.

In the passage you read, Jews and Gentiles had assembled after long travels to follow Jesus. They were desperate to receive something from Jesus. While their rations were gone, one meal would not have necessarily sustained everyone for their return journeys home, especially not the children. The tangible expressions of Christ's compassion (cups of water and food) won't last forever; they are shadows of the perfect love and compassion Christ showed us on the cross.

Read John 6:26-36.

> *What did the crowd seek from Jesus?*

> *Jesus knew what they really needed. He gave them physical compassion, but how did He respond to their request for more bread?*

> *When do you find yourself seeking only the tangible expressions of Christ's compassion and neglecting the spiritual ones?*

In the passage, Messianic expectations clouded the crowds' understanding of Jesus' willingness to give. We can make the same mistake today—seeking only what God can give, instead of seeking Him.

> *Read Romans 5:8, and copy the words in the space below:*

This is God's ultimate act of love to us, and it is far greater than a loaf of bread or a cup of water. Based on our sinful state, there is nothing we deserve from the hand of God. Thankfully He freely gives to all. Close in prayer using the following to guide you:

- What is your biggest physical need today? Ask God to provide according to His will.

- What is your biggest spiritual need today? Ask God to fill You.

- Ask God to help you put more focus on the spiritual, the everlasting bread of life, and not just on the temporary, the bread on your plate.

INDIVIDUAL STUDY: DAY THREE

Ask God to awaken in your heart His mission for believers. Use the prayer below as a guide:

God, by the powerful presence of Your Holy Spirit, stir in me a renewed sense of Your mission to live out the compassionate, forgiving, life-giving love of Jesus in a world that desperately needs an accurate picture of your Son. Help me to see people as You see them and to sow seeds of faith in my relationships so that others see You. Amen.

Read Matthew 11 in its entirety.

This chapter focuses on a man on God's mission. The chapter begins with John in prison, doubting his ministry of declaring Christ because of his arrest and possibly doubting his own beliefs about the Messiah. Through an exchange with messengers, Jesus affirmed His call and John's mission by reminding John of the Old Testament prophecies the Lord was fulfilling. Each one affirms God's promises and also indicates the way Christ engaged compassionately with people.

> **Look back at Matthew 11:4-5 and make a list of those illustrations of compassion in the space provided.**

Jesus then addressed the crowd, speaking kindly regarding John but also warning of the danger of rejecting the message about Him. He concluded His discourse with famous words of rest and encouragement in Matthew 11:28-30.

> **Copy the words of Jesus from these verses in the space below:**

> **Write briefly what these words mean to you.**

Matthew 11:28-30 is evidence of Christ's compassion.

Compassionate words to an afflicted slave.

Compassionate words to a faithful servant in prison.

Compassionate words to us today.

Matthew 11:28-30 is a cup of cold water at just the right moment.

From what circumstances does your heart need rest today?

Ask God for His perfect rest. Lay your burdens at His feet.
Write a prayer to God in the space below.

What do you think Jesus meant when He said His yoke is easy?
Do you ever find it difficult to follow Jesus?

It's clear in the passage you read today that following Jesus is not always easy. John was in prison when Jesus spoke these words. The idea of "taking a yoke" is a metaphor for becoming a disciple. Submission to Christ is being yoked to Him. In this context, the word "easy" literally means "well-fitting." Being yoked to Jesus is "tailor-made for our lives and needs."[4]

What a comforting thought. Jesus is the perfect fit. Be it a difficult situation in your workplace, school, marriage, or community. Be it a personal struggle with temptation, addiction, or burden of sin. Be it a consequence of your actions or a byproduct of the actions of others in your life. Be it a challenge with your children or an intense season of grief. He is the perfect fit for you.

As you close this session, pray specifically for each of the items below:

- Thank God for the death of Jesus on the cross—His ultimate act of compassion.

- Thank Him for His daily expressions of compassion in your life.

- Thank Him today for soul rest.

- Ask Him again to help you be a herald of that compassion and a signpost to those around you who need the love of Jesus.

BEN-HUR
Session Three

ENCOUNTER WITH A CHRIST WHO SUFFERED

The cross was on the other back. Jesus, our Lord and Savior, hung on the cross, bearing the sins of the world. Judah Ben-Hur encounters Jesus for the third time as Jesus suffered. This moment with Jesus ultimately leads to Judah's salvation experience. Christ's suffering paid the price for our own salvation, and it's the reason we must take the love of Christ to the world.

From then on Jesus began to point out to His disciples that He must go to Jerusalem and suffer many things from the elders, chief priests, and scribes, be killed, and be raised the third day. (Matt. 16:21)

GATHER

Welcome to week three. Think back to your individual study from week two. This week, how have you seen Jesus' compassion:

- In your own life or in your family?

- In a friend?

- In the news or other media outlets?

- In your church?

- Through other believers?

Discuss the following to begin your group study today:

What do you like most about being a Christian?

How could a believer possibly get caught up with only seeking the blessings of Christ and not Christ Himself?

What role do you think suffering plays in the life of a Christian?

How do you remind yourself to see the bigger picture of what Christ did and connect with the person of Jesus, instead of just seeking comfort from Him?

Our salvation and eternal relationship with Christ started at that moment on the cross in Jesus' time of fiercest pain. To identify with Jesus as a believer is to identify with Him in His suffering.

How does the fact that Jesus endured such great suffering affect your view of His love?

How does Christ's love inspire you to show love to others?

As you begin this week's study, remember the connection between Christ's love and His suffering. While Jesus was fully divine, He was also completely human. His suffering was real, and yet His willingness to endure offers us a picture of God's purpose and a powerful demonstration of true compassion.

WATCH

As a group, view the week three teaching video with Greg Laurie. Read the summary below before watching the video. Then discuss the teaching video together using the questions provided.

Summary:

In this segment, Greg Laurie summarizes the scene where Judah Ben-Hur encounters Christ for the third time as Christ is on His way to the cross. Laurie reminds us of Judah's desire for revenge. In the film, Jesus comforts Judah with the words of John 10:18, saying about His life, "I lay it down on my own." No one took Christ's life from Him; He gave it freely. The work of salvation occurred thousands of years ago, but it comes instantly as a person crosses over from death to life. The film shows us that moment for Judah. When Ben-Hur drops the rock, his vengeance drops along with it. His life is forever changed.

Discuss:

1. *Christ was not alone when He was crucified. Based on the teaching video, what crimes did the men hanging beside Jesus commit? How did they respond to Jesus? How did Jesus respond?*

2. *How often do you contemplate the great suffering and pain Jesus endured on the cross? Visual depictions like the one in Ben-Hur can help us connect with this significant moment in salvation history. How do those depictions make you feel?*

3. *Jesus gave Judah a cup of cold water once, and Judah returned the favor as best he could when Jesus was on His way to the cross. How can believers follow this example and "give a cup of water" to Jesus today?*

ENGAGE

Examine the passages of Scripture on the left of the chart as a group and fill in the corresponding questions for each.

Based on the prophecy, how would Jesus suffer?
How was this prophecy fulfilled?

Psalm 41:7-9: _____ (see Mark 14:10-11)

Zechariah 13:7: _____ (see Matt. 26:31)

Isaiah 50:6: _____ (see Matt. 27:26-30)

Isaiah 53:4-11: _____ (see John 19:16-19)

Look back at Isaiah 53:4-11. List all the words used to describe Jesus' suffering in this passage:

Why did Jesus have to die?

Read the quote below from John Piper about the suffering of Jesus and its relationship to the salvation from God and the sovereignty of God. Circle every reference to Christ's suffering.

"But God was not willing to leave us in this guilty and condemned condition. He planned from ages past to send a Suffering Servant, not mainly to model love for us, but to bear our sins as a substitute for us. 'The Lord has laid on him the iniquity of us all.' This is the heart of Christianity. Jesus Christ came into the world to fulfill this prophecy—yes, many others to be sure, but this one is central and basic. He came to die. He came to die in our place. He came to die for our sins. This is our only hope."[1]

According to Piper, the suffering of Christ accomplished two distinct things for us. Complete the statements below.

Jesus came to _____ in our place.

Jesus' death _____ provides our only _____.

Christ was not spared suffering. We can't avoid suffering either. The gospel message is that He suffered freely in our place to bring us salvation. That was God's plan all along.

This is perhaps the most important question you will answer during this study:

Have you placed your faith in Jesus Christ for your salvation? If you answered no, reach out to someone in your group, and ask them to tell you how you can receive this grace from Jesus. If you answered yes, pray for others you know who haven't yet surrendered to Jesus as Lord.

INDIVIDUAL STUDY: DAY ONE

In your personal study this week, you will look at several eyewitnesses to Jesus' final hours before His death.

To begin, make a simple list of various authority figures in your life.

Do you find it easy to submit to authority, or do you sometimes find yourself resisting them? Explain.

Read the following accounts of Jesus' crucifixion from the Gospels, and answer the questions that follow.

Matthew 27:27-31, Mark 15:16-20, Luke 23:6-12, John 19:1-4

List any details that are repeated in all or several of the Gospel accounts.

Which account differs the most from the others?

The Roman soldiers in each account were men acting under authority. Being a good soldier meant explicitly carrying out orders. Vulgar and unfeeling as they were, these men merely carried out the direct orders of their commanders. By God's sovereignty and their own cruelty, they fulfilled God's prophecies.

Now transition from the group of soldiers to a single Centurion present at Jesus' death.

Read Matthew 27:45-54.

Scripture tells us the centurion and those with him witnessed miraculous events, sparking his declaration that Christ must truly be the Son of God as He claimed.

In addition to the earthquake, look through the passage and list the miracles Scripture records.

How would you react to seeing these miracles take place?

The soldiers who flogged Jesus were numb to execution. To them it was another day, another direct order, and another death on the books. But for the centurion at the close of Matthew 27, something else happened: *Transformation*. He had seen crucifixion before, but there must have been something different about this one. Jesus' temperament? Perhaps. His words? Maybe. The sudden darkness? For sure. He responded in faith to Jesus and declared Him truly to be God's Son.

Let's take a look at one more person who encountered Jesus in His final hours. Read each passage below and note the similarities and differences between each account.

Matthew 27:32:

Mark 15:21:

Luke 23:26:

Did this man carry Jesus' cross willingly?

Scripture provides only minor details of Simon the Cyrenian, but there is one simple fact of which we can be sure. The soldiers forced him to carry Christ's cross.

In contrast, recall John 10:18 from this week's group study. Did anyone force Christ to bear the pain of the cross? Could any earthly power hold Him there?

Christ gave His life of His own will and authority. Simon the Cyrenian was forced to carry Christ's physical cross, but God does not force us to believe in Him. Instead, He invites us. We don't know what happened to Simon, or if he ever believed in Jesus as Savior. But carrying Christ's cross under strict orders is not the same as trusting Christ's work on the cross at the invitation of the Holy Spirit.

While God does not force us to believe in Christ, as followers of Jesus we are commanded to take up our cross.

Read Mark 8:34-35.

What do you think it means to take up your cross as you follow Jesus?

What is Jesus' prescription for people who want to save their lives?

Close your time today by examining your heart and motivation for following Jesus. Do you go to church out of guilt or obligation? Do you read your Bible to check it off your list or out of a desire to know Christ more intimately? Are you willingly and joyfully following Christ? Pray and ask God to make these desires present in your life.

INDIVIDUAL STUDY: DAY TWO

Have you ever heard the phrase, "an inconvenient truth?" Today we will look at a man in Scripture who faced a most inconvenient truth and eventually made the decision that sent Christ to the cross.

Read Matthew 27:11-26.

> *Describe Pilate's struggle between what he had heard of Jesus and what he experienced of Jesus firsthand.*

Consider Pilate's dilemma. To declare oneself king was treason. Technically, Jesus never admitted such to Pilate in the Gospel of Matthew. At the encouragement of his wife, Pilate did what he could to avoid crucifying Jesus, ultimately washing his hands of the offense.

Caught between his responsibility to Rome and keeping the Sanhedrin quiet, Pilate faced several inconvenient truths.

1. Was Jesus the Son of God?

2. Was Jesus guilty of any crime?

3. Why allow the release of a known criminal like Barabbas?

4. What should he do with regard to his wife's dream and Jesus' blood?

In this situation, Pilate had to act as judge.

> *Have you ever been in a position of authority when you had to judge someone's actions, beliefs, and motivations? What was it like? If not, how difficult do you think it would be to serve in such a position?*

> *Have you ever been pressured to act in a way that contradicted what you believed to be true? How did you respond?*

Hindsight doesn't hold Pilate responsible for Jesus' death. Crucifixion was God's plan. However, Pilate, like all of us, is responsible for his encounter with Jesus' truth.

Throughout this study you have put yourself in the sandals of Judah Ben-Hur. Betrayed by a friend. Innocent, yet convicted. Beaten and enslaved. Fearful for your family and your future. Fueled by revenge. Changed by a connection to Christ Jesus.

Now put yourself in Pilate's sandals. Placed in a position of authority. Pressured politically by the empire, socially by the crowds, and emotionally from your own spouse. Fearful of making a mistake. More fearful of enduring the consequences religiously, economically, politically, and relationally. What was Pilate to do with such inconvenience, truth or not?

What biblical truth have you struggled with recently? How is that teaching of Jesus difficult to obey?

What do you do with such truths? Look for the loopholes? Wash your hands of them altogether? Obey even when you don't understand? Or do you ask and wait for God to show you His wisdom and power?

If Pilate had accepted the truth right in front of him, he would have stopped Jesus' execution, forfeiting salvation for us all. Mercifully, that wasn't part of God's plan. If Judah Ben-Hur had ignored the truth in front of him, he would have persisted in his anger, lived for his revenge, been eaten alive by his hate, and ultimately missed the message of forgiveness Jesus lived and died communicating.

If you are guilty of ignoring part of God's truth, how can you obey God's command to share the truth of Christ's sacrifice with others?

If you are not yet a follower of Jesus and still exploring the Bible's claims, consider what it means for you to ignore Christ. If He is indeed who Scripture says He is, offering the Salvation that Scripture says only He can, then what would missing that truth mean for you?

Will you try to ignore the truth, or will you press in and believe in faith? Pray and ask God for strength to choose His truth in a world that eagerly accepts compromise.

INDIVIDUAL STUDY: DAY THREE

In today's personal study, you'll look at the story of a dying criminal who encountered Jesus during His last hours of life. To start this section, examine your heart and answer the questions below.

Do you rejoice when you hear of someone giving their life to Christ in faith? Why or why not?

How do you react when you witness baptism—the symbol of someone's salvation and new life in Jesus?

How do you react to stories of people on death row becoming Christians? Do you raise a suspicious eyebrow or feel conflicted about a certain "level" of sinners declaring repentance?

As you dive into your Scripture study today, remember the tax collector from session one, and God's ability to redeem even the most "unredeemable." To begin, read Isaiah's prophecy about Christ being crucified among criminals and underline each appearance of the word "rebels" in the verse.

> **Therefore I will give Him the many as a portion, and He will receive the mighty as spoil, because He submitted Himself to death, and was counted among the rebels; yet He bore the sin of many and interceded for the rebels. (Isaiah 53:12)**

Now read the account of the "rebels" crucified with Christ in Luke 23:32-43.

While many modern day renditions of Christ's crucifixion refer to the criminals as thieves, it's unlikely that Rome would have used such a cruel punishment for a simple robber. Because Isaiah prophesied "rebels," Greg Laurie is probably right to assume that the men were Zealots.

Record the statements the repentant criminal made on the cross both to his fellow captive and to Jesus.

What do the convict's statements indicate about his heart?

People sometimes think they have to clean up their lives before they can come to Christ or even to church. How does this passage contradict that idea?

Now read the following verses about life for Christ-followers. List the specific characteristics that these passages explain will indicate believers.

2 Corinthians 5:17-21:

Colossians 3:12-17:

Were any of these characteristics present in the criminal's life between the time he put his faith in Jesus and the time he died?

Hours from his own death, this converted criminal had no time left to break in his new clothes and represent his new Savior. A missional life wasn't possible or necessary. The suffering work of Christ on the cross accomplished the criminal's salvation fully and completely.

Christ was truly the suffering servant. In His own final hours on earth, He extended grace to a condemned man, transferring him from death to life.

Christ's sacrifice didn't only demonstrate God's love. It saved sinners from death, even those who wouldn't walk in newness of life *in* Christ until they walked in resurrected life *with* Christ.

In closing, read Paul's testimony in 1 Timothy 1:15-16.

Who did Jesus come to save?

How does Paul refer to himself in this passage?

In verse 16, what is Paul's explanation for why Christ showed him mercy?

Ask God to increase your burden for the lost. Is there someone or some sin you view as outside the bounds of Christ's miracle-working forgiveness? Ask God to replace the stony parts of your heart with His flesh. Thank God for showing patience to you, a sinner, and ask Him to extend that patience to others through you. Thank Him for His immense suffering for sinners like you.

BEN-HUR
Session Four

ENCOUNTER WITH A PERSON CHRIST CHANGED

Judah Ben-Hur came home a changed man. Years of slavery and abuse will do that to a person. So will a tiny seed of anger as it grows into a mighty oak of revenge in a person's soul. When he encounters Esther, a woman he once loved, she has also been changed by Jesus and offers Judah a message of hope he hasn't yet considered.

> **But how can they call on Him they have not believed in? And how can they believe without hearing about Him? And how can they hear without a preacher? And how can they preach unless they are sent? As it is written: How beautiful are the feet of those who announce the gospel of good things! (Rom. 10:14-15)**

GATHER

Welcome to week four. Begin this week by sharing portions of your individual study experience from week three. Use the following questions as your guide:

> **What stood out most to you during last week's group discussion or devotional studies?**

> **How did you see God's grace at work in your life this week?**

Reread 2 Corinthians 5:17 below from this past week's personal study.

Therefore, if anyone is in Christ, he is a new creation; old things have passed away, and look, new things have come.

> **What "old things" need to pass away when we put our faith in Christ?**

> **What "new things" do you think should consistently come into the lives of all believers?**

Share with each other how you have witnessed those "new things" played out in one another's lives.

Did evangelism make your list of "new things?" The desire to share Christ with others is born out of your joy in finding Christ. Read the following definition of evangelism out loud.

"Evangelism is one beggar telling another beggar where to find bread." D.T. Niles[1]

> **Put this quote into your own words.**

As a group, make evangelism a priority. If you feel comfortable, share the names of people in your circles of influence who do not know Christ. Pray for opportunities to share the good news of Jesus with those you named.

Make this your prayer this week: *Lord, may our affection for You and the joy of what we have found in You cause us to share You with others who need You. Amen.*

WATCH

As a group, view the week four teaching video with Greg Laurie. Read the summary below before watching the video. Then discuss the teaching video together using the questions provided.

Summary:

Greg Laurie references the scene between Esther and Judah Ben-Hur where she explains to Judah what she has come to believe about Jesus of Nazareth. Chronologically, this scene takes place prior to the scene between Judah and Christ that we discussed in session three. In this teaching segment, Laurie reminds us as believers of the responsibility we bear to share the good news of Jesus. Some believers merely treat Christ's Great Commission (Matt. 28:19-20) as a really good suggestion, and many other believers have eliminated it from their faith practice altogether as if it were a great omission.

Discuss:

1. *Is there a particular piece of the teaching segment that stood out most to you? What was it?*

2. *Judah Ben-Hur told Esther that faith didn't keep him alive because it wasn't strong enough. Are there moments when you consider your faith too weak to share? Why or why not?*

3. *Who do you know who is lonely and searching for answers? How have you attempted to tell them about Jesus?*

4. *Laurie explains that our mission is to build bridges, not burn them. Does fear of saying the wrong thing ever keep you from evangelizing? What can you do to overcome that fear?*

ENGAGE

In today's group time, you will discover three crucial truths about evangelism.

Truth #1: The world needs to hear. Read Matthew 24:14 and Acts 2:39.

> *How much do you think about the end times? What could result from focusing too much or not enough?*

> *How are the end times related to evangelism?*

The world needs to hear the good news of Jesus because one day the world will end. The Bible says none of us are promised tomorrow (James 4:14), so our spirit of urgency should be high. People are far from God (Acts 2:39), and evangelism brings them one step closer.

Truth #2: Someone must tell them. Read Romans 10:13-17.

> *Describe the sense of urgency in this passage.*

> *Will everyone who hears determine Christ is Lord and turn to Him in faith for salvation? (See Rom. 10:16)*

> *How has fear of rejection ever kept you from sharing your faith with others?*

This passage uses Israel's rejection of the Messiah to highlight Paul's ministry to the Gentiles. God used Paul to take the message of Christ to the Gentiles. He can use you to take the same gospel message across the street or around the world.

Truth #3: Sharing should be our joy. Read 1 John 1:3-4 and Acts 20:35.

> *Share a time when you found great joy in pointing someone to Jesus.*

There is great joy for believers in knowing and following Christ, and there is great joy in watching Christ come alive in others. Greg Laurie writes in his Bible study, *Tell Someone,* that the happiest Christians are those who are evangelistic Christians, those whose attentions are focused on fulfilling the Great Commission. Conversely, the most unhappy Christians are the most nit-picky Christians, those who are too busy arguing within to focus their attention outward missionally.[2]

Turn your attention outward today. Who needs to hear the gospel? Will God use you to tell them? Pray for boldness in sharing your faith with those who are still far from God.

INDIVIDUAL STUDY: DAY ONE

In this week of personal study, you will explore individual encounters with Jesus that led people to share with others both the good news of Jesus and the personal joy they found in Him.

Define evangelism in your own words using the space provided.

Evangelism is:

To get in the right frame of mind for today's study, take a minute to recall a few important details of your own discovery in Christ.

What faith-sharing studies, exercises, programs, or tools have you participated in previously?

How did those opportunities shape the way you engage others with the good news of Jesus?

We talk a lot about the "message" of the gospel. You may have used that word in your definition. Write out the message God calls us to share.

In the scene Greg Laurie referenced this week, Jesus is not present, but is still very much alive. It's a pre-crucifixion moment. Esther believes Jesus is the Messiah, and her life has been changed by Christ, but Christ has not yet risen from the dead.

Read Romans 10:8-9.

What confession of faith does Paul prescribe in Romans 10:9 that Esther was not able to make yet in the film?

Now you will take a look at one woman's encounter with a post-resurrection Jesus. Read each of the following passages, and note what each says about Mary Magdalene.

Luke 8:1-3:

Matthew 27:55-56:

Mark 16:1-3:

Scripture doesn't give us many details about this woman. Although it's commonly believed she may have been a woman of poor reputation, nothing in Scripture directly links her to the sinful woman caught in adultery. Mary Magdalene began following Jesus after He healed her from demon possession (Luke 8:1-3). Along with other women, she stayed close by after Jesus' death. She is mentioned in each of the four Gospels as one of the women who discovered the empty tomb.[3]

Read John's account of the empty tomb in John 20:11-18 to get a glimpse of her encounter with the risen, victorious Jesus.

In the space below, write down the questions Jesus asked Mary Magdalene in John's account.

Next, write the instructions Jesus gave to Mary Magdalene at the tomb.

What did Mary Magdalene do following Jesus' instructions?

Mary obeyed her Lord. She immediately went and pronounced to the disciples, "I have seen the Lord" (John 20:18) and told them what He had said to her. Essentially, Mary shared her testimony.

A testimony is simply telling about one's experience. Mary's testimony in this moment was having seen the risen Lord. Have you shared your testimony about Jesus recently?

Note the moment when Mary mistook Jesus for a gardener. His resurrected body was different. The Jesus she knew and followed had changed. The beaten Lord she lamented over was restored. Just as Jesus' resurrection changed His physical form, our belief in His resurrection changes our spiritual form. And our testimonies about our experiences with Jesus can change lives.

Close in prayer by meditating on your own testimony, thanking God for bringing you to this place in your journey with Christ.

INDIVIDUAL STUDY: DAY TWO

Today you will examine the experience of two men who walked and talked with the resurrected Lord. Read Luke 24:13-35.

> *What feelings of discouragement must have overcome these disciples as they traveled north from Jerusalem to their town of Emmaus? Why were they so distraught?*

When you consider their disbelief, it can be frustrating. What more did these gentlemen need? They had a front row seat to the events of the week and knew many details of Jesus' life and ministry. They also had the testimony of the women who reported the empty tomb.

> *In verse 27, what did Jesus use to answer their questions initially regarding His suffering?*

> *What finally occurred to open their eyes to the truth of Christ standing before them (verse 30)?*

> *What moment in Christ's passion week did this event reflect?*

> *What did they do after Jesus vanished from their sight?*

As they were telling the others about their encounter on the road, Jesus appeared in their midst a second time. Read Luke 24:44-49.

> *What did Jesus say would happen beginning in Jerusalem (verse 47)?*

These men witnessed the most miraculous events in human history. They physically saw Jesus' ministry, death and His resurrected body.

> *In light of all they had seen, what was their responsibility?*

Have you heard this quote before? "With great power comes great responsibility." Did you know it has roots in Scripture?

Much will be required of everyone who has been given much. And even more will be expected of the one who has been entrusted with more. (Luke 12:48)

You may not have been given the chance to see Jesus in the flesh, but if you are indeed a follower of Jesus, you have the responsibility and privilege of representing Him every day in your circle of influence.

Use the diagram below to identify your circles of influence. The smallest, inner circle represents your personal struggles in life. Inside this circle, write issues that take your focus off of Christ. The larger, outer circle represents the areas of your life where you have influence and can spread the good news. Write inside of this circle the names of people who need you to pray for or share the gospel with them.

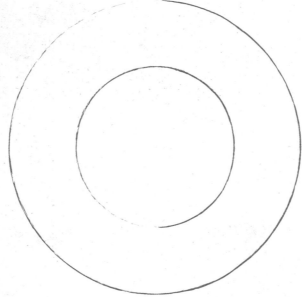

One of the reasons the disciples did not recognize Jesus on the road to Emmaus was because they were inwardly focused instead of outwardly focused. They were too concerned with their unmet expectations to see that Scripture had been fulfilled right before their eyes.

The more you focus on your primary call as a believer, to seek God first, the concerns in the inner circle will diminish and need less of your attention. Then you will have more capacity to look outside your own needs and turn your attention to others. Part of seeking God first is living your faith in a contagious, expressive way. Close today with this quote from Greg Laurie's study, *Tell Someone.* Make these words your declaration.

"Lives are at stake. I am positioned strategically to influence others in order to see them saved from death and given eternal life. Step out. Take a risk. It's worth it. I have good news that will change everything."[4]

INDIVIDUAL STUDY: DAY THREE

Today, as you begin your study, dive immediately into prayer asking the God of this great universe to speak directly to you and grant you specific wisdom regarding His will. Use the prayer below as a guide.

Holy God, open my eyes. Open my mind and heart to Your will and Your ways. Help me to sense and seize Your wisdom. Use my relationship with You and make me a light in this world for those who don't yet know that there is a God in Heaven who loves them and sent His only Son to die in their places. Change me, and challenge me, God. Amen.

Read the following two accounts from the Apostle Paul's life and testimony before Christ, and answer the questions that follow.

Read Acts 8:1-3 and Acts 9:1-2.

Describe Saul's actions and attitudes toward Christians in these passages.

According to Acts 8:2, what happened to the believers who faced persecution at Saul's hand? What two regions are specifically named?

Ironically, the persecution meant to stifle Christianity actually helped to spread the early Christians to regions beyond Jerusalem. Saul's persecution helped fulfill the words Christ spoke before His ascension in Acts 1:8; His followers would be His witnesses "in Jerusalem, in all Judea and Samaria, and to the ends of the earth."

Have you ever experienced persecution (even if not to the degree of these early believers) because of your faith in Christ? How did you respond?

On his way to seize additional Christ followers in Damascus, Saul experienced a dramatic conversion experience. Read Paul's encounter with the Lord in Acts 9:3-19 and answer the questions that follow.

How did Ananias respond to the Lord's instructions?

If you had been Paul, how do you think you would have responded to the Lord?

The man responsible for early persecution in the church would one day be persecuted on behalf of new churches. Now read the following account of Paul's post-conversion life describing the details of his life's mission in Christ.

Read Romans 15:14-21.

Complete the sentence below to summarize this passage into one comprehensive mission statement for Paul's ministry.

Paul's mission was to _____.

Read Isaiah 52:15. Which statement did Paul make in Romans 15 that references these words from Isaiah?

In what context have you proclaimed God's truth to people and places who do not yet know Him?

Even if it's not possible for you to physically go and share the gospel with people who have never heard, how can you be part of God's mission to proclaim salvation to the ends of the earth?

Close your time today by considering Paul's mission to be your own. The Great Commission of Jesus (Matt. 28:19-20) is a command for all believers to go and make disciples of all nations, teaching them to observe the words of God. Ask God to reveal to you a plan for you to communicate His truth in your current context to people far from Him. Just as God physically opened Paul's eyes from his blindness, ask God to open your eyes to His purposes for you. Perhaps God will give you ears to hear and a heart to obey Him with these new opportunities to share His truth.

Write down 3 specific ways you feel God is leading you to take action and be obedient to His call to make disciples of all nations:

1.

2.

3.

BEN-HUR

Session Five

ENCOUNTER WITH THE FORGIVENESS OF JESUS

When salvation comes to a house, the spirit and aroma of the house are changed. With salvation comes forgiveness from God to us and from us to others. Ben-Hur believed and received forgiveness. A newly faith-filled Ben-Hur then faces Messala, the man who wronged Ben-Hur and whom Ben-Hur has wronged. The outcome? Forgiveness.

And be kind and compassionate to one another, forgiving one another, just as God also forgave you in Christ. (Eph. 4:32)

GATHER

Welcome to week five. Begin this group time by sharing something interesting from your individual study experience. Use the following questions as a guide:

How did God speak to you this week through your personal Bible study?

Did you have any opportunities to talk about Christ's love with people in your circles of influence this week?

You ended your personal study last time by looking at the life of Paul—persecutor turned missionary. Read Paul's words in Romans 15:7-9 and circle the words in this passage associated with forgiveness.

Therefore accept one another, just as the Messiah also accepted you, to the glory of God. For I say that the Messiah became a servant of the circumcised on behalf of God's truth, to confirm the promises to the fathers, and so that Gentiles may glorify God for His mercy.

What words did you circle?

These verses contain two significant words to examine in light of this week's encounter with Christ. If you didn't already, circle the words "accept" and "mercy."

To accept is to take one in and offer friendship.[1] How is that a picture of the forgiveness we've received from Christ for our sins?

Mercy is kindness to the afflicted. It means withholding the death and punishment man deserves and offering gracious salvation from God instead.[2]

Christ set the example and accepted us in His mercy even when we were sinners. How should we respond? How does God's mercy affect how you show kindness?

WATCH

As a group, view the week five teaching video with Greg Laurie. Read the summary below before watching the video. Then discuss the teaching video together using the questions provided.

Summary:

Greg Laurie reminds us in this video that forgiven people are forgiving people. Ben-Hur saw Jesus die on the cross and heard Jesus' words of forgiveness. Judah Ben-Hur's past was full of resentment. If he continued to carry it, he would always remain a victim. Judah Ben-Hur, having experienced Christ's forgiveness, extends forgiveness to Messala.

Discuss:

1. **In the scene Greg Laurie discussed, what is the symbolism of Messala dropping the dagger? How is this similar to Ben-Hur dropping his rock?**

2. **What happens when we hold on to bitterness? Who is the more injured party?**

3. **How does Christ's forgiveness prompt you to be more forgiving to others?**

4. **Who are you harboring resentment toward? Who are you having difficulty forgiving?**

ENGAGE

Read Ephesians 4:32.

According to this verse, why are we commanded to forgive one another?

How has forgiveness been a positive experience in your life?

What do you find most difficult about seeking and giving forgiveness?

Consider your own need for forgiveness. We know we need God's forgiveness for our sin, but we also need forgiveness from others. Is it easy for you to accept forgiveness from others? Are you quick to offer excuses for your behavior? How do you respond when others offer similar excuses? Do you tend to reject them or attempt to understand them?

Read Jesus' parable about forgiveness in Matthew 18:23-35.

Compare the debt the slave owed to the debt his fellow slave owed him. Which was the greater debt?

Whether small offenses or large grievances, there is nothing outside the bounds of God's forgiveness. Why? Because Christ's death was complete. There is no sin for which Jesus' suffering was insufficient.[3]

Why would the servant in the parable turn around and be so wicked after receiving such a great gift?

Perhaps the servant was only glad to be off the hook and not fully walking in the reality of the debt that his master had just removed from him.

Is there a difference between absolving guilt and being forgiven? If so, what is it?

When we understand how much we've been forgiven and come face-to-face with how much it cost, we naturally want to take care of the message that comes with it.

Close with prayer for one another. Ask God to move in your heart this week. A rock or a dagger might drop in your life. An illustration of God's faithfulness, Christ's sacrifice, and the Spirit's power might just be one page turn away in your story.

INDIVIDUAL STUDY: DAY ONE

Let your fingers do some walking at the start of this week's personal study. Thumb through the previous four weeks of devotions, and recall the many encounters various people in the gospels had with Jesus. Some were named individuals with many details. Some were unnamed people about whom we know very little. Some were groups or vast crowds. In some, you dissected Messianic expectations and evaluated what it means to seek Jesus. In some, you witnessed miracles and were given glimpses of Christ's compassion. In others, you saw the birth of their belief and watched them embrace their call to share Jesus without hesitation.

Which character or encounter stood out the most to you over the past few weeks of study?

The final three encounters you'll have this week focus on forgiveness. In some ways, since you have already seen Jesus at the crucifixion and the resurrection, you'll be moving backwards toward where you started this study with Jesus' earthly ministry.

Since we live 2,000 years after the death, resurrection, and ascension of Jesus, we are always moving back and forth over the biblical landscape. As you do, remember the importance of seeing every story in light of the gospel story. Whether it is the Old Testament before Christ came or the New Testament before He died—everything you experience in Scripture is better understood in light of an empty tomb and a risen Savior.

Read Matthew 9:1-7 and answer the questions that follow.

List the cast of characters Jesus encounters in this story.

Why does each one seek Jesus?

What phrase does Jesus use in performing this miracle, and why was it problematic?

What reason does Jesus give for this statement?

How does the crowd respond to the miracle?

The healing of a man who couldn't walk showed God's power. People saw with their own eyes the proof of this miracle. The forgiveness of sins before God was not as easy to prove, so Jesus effectively killed two birds with one stone. God is incredible at multi-tasking. Jesus used the physical proof of the healing to validate the Son of Man's authority to forgive sins. People who rejected Jesus as Messiah found it problematic that He would dare speak for God. The miracle alerted the crowds following Jesus that His miracles weren't just appropriate in this kingdom but sufficient for the next as well.[1]

This miracle was an invitation for people to see Jesus in a new light. He didn't just have access to help from God; He could access the very Kingdom of God. It invited people to seek Jesus for more than just physical miracles and instead look to Him for a message of saving hope and faith.

What proof has God given you in your life or in your faith community to illustrate His authority and sovereign power?

How do these proofs spark obedience and worship in your life?

Where do you need God's power most in your life today? Is it a physical need or a spiritual ailment? Close in prayer, thanking God for both His authority and willingness to forgive. Write down three or four areas in your life where you need His forgiveness and healing.

INDIVIDUAL STUDY: DAY TWO

Lew Wallace's original novel *Ben-Hur* included a peculiar tag line. While the story centered on Wallace's fictional Jewish prince, Judah Ben-Hur, he tagged the book: "A Tale of the Christ." Perhaps Wallace's intent was to show that the Christ-follower's story really ought to be the story of Jesus Christ. When we live our lives in light of Christ's death and resurrection, we're truly living a bigger story.

Begin your study today with the story of someone whose sins were forgiven in dramatic fashion.

Read John 8:1-11.

Who was forgiven in this story, and what was the sin?

What did the earthly authorities want to do regarding this woman's sin?

What was different about Jesus' plan?

How did the others in the passage respond to Jesus' offering of forgiveness?

Why do you think her accusers left that day without following through with their law?

What did the woman gain that day in addition to Jesus' offering of forgiveness?

How do you think the offering of forgiveness affected the woman?

Note the following facts that would have been true surrounding this scenario:

- To be caught in the act of adultery would have required a second party. Where was the man? The law of Moses required both be stoned. (See Lev. 20:10)

- To stone the woman would have cost Jesus His growing status as a friend of sinners. To neglect the stoning would have made Him a lawbreaker. By earthly standards, Jesus appeared to have been caught in a conundrum.

- We do not know what Jesus wrote on the ground. Some scholars indicate that His actions could have reminded the Pharisees that the Ten Commandments were written by the very finger of God.[5] (see Ex. 31:18)

Jesus was not being dismissive of sin by interacting with a woman caught breaking a sacred Old Testament command. He was simply offering her the forgiveness His death would soon purchase. While consumer debt is rarely a good idea, consider this action of Jesus similar to the "buy now, pay later" approach credit card companies promote. The woman walked away that day with a free offer of forgiveness, but Christ would very soon pay the high price for her sins. Jesus' death doesn't eliminate the consequence of sin; it satisfies the demands of it.

Ultimately, forgiveness is not free.

What does that statement mean to you?

The woman's accusers left, but the accusation remained. She was guilty according to the law of God. All of us are. Jesus didn't determine that her crime no longer carried the status of sin or no longer deserved the consequence of it. Instead, He offered to suffer in her stead.

Did the woman do anything to earn Jesus' forgiveness?

Think about the teaching video from your group study this week. Did Messala do anything to earn forgiveness from Judah Ben-Hur? No, he threatened him with death. Forgiveness isn't based on the person being forgiven. It's based on the one forgiving.

When God forgives a sinner, it's because the price has already been paid.

As you close this session, write a prayer expressing your gratitude for Christ's forgiveness and the high price He paid for our sins. Thank Him for paying your debt in full.

INDIVIDUAL STUDY: DAY THREE

Read Luke 23:32-37. You studied this passage during week three, but today you will focus on the words of Jesus. Identify the characters in the passage, and list their actions or reactions to Jesus on the chart below.

Character   *Actions / Reactions to Jesus*

_____   _____

_____   _____

_____   _____

_____   _____

_____   _____

In the space below, copy Jesus' exact words found in Luke 23:34.

What were the soldiers' words in Luke 23:37?

If those men understood what Jesus was doing, they wouldn't have mockingly asserted He save Himself. They would have wept, thanking Jesus for saving them.

Think of people who are antagonistic to faith in Christ and closed to the forgiveness of sin found only in Jesus. Why do you think they refuse to hear the message of grace through faith in Christ?

Perhaps their refusal to believe in Jesus comes from their unwillingness to recognize sin in this world and in their own lives, or perhaps it comes from a bad experience with churches or other believers.

Describe the values and behaviors of people who reject the truth of Christ. What are their perceptions of Christianity? What do they say and believe about Jesus?

As sinners saved by grace, mere beggars ourselves, it's easy to become frustrated by the actions and attitudes of the ungodly because they so contradict the message of truth and the way of life we're called to adopt.

How do you respond when someone is negative or hostile toward Christianity?

As believers, we have two options: judgment or forgiveness. Like Jesus, His followers ought to be able to look at the depravity in the world and repeat His words, "Father, forgive them, because they do not know what they are doing" (Luke 23:34).

If criminals, terrorists, and worldly idealists understood the truth of why Jesus died, they would not mock Jesus with their lives. Instead, they would tearfully and joyfully respond to grace with gratitude for salvation.

It goes a step further. If judgmental, dismissive people who claim to be Christ-followers truly grasped the reason Christ died and the price of forgiveness, they would be able to join Him in His suffering, look at the world around them, and lovingly proclaim, *Father, forgive them. They just don't know.*

And with that burden, we'll feel compelled to go and tell them.

In this study, you encountered a carpenter who spoke of an eternal Kingdom.

You encountered Christ with a message of hope and willing to suffer.

You encountered a transformed woman with a message and a freed man willing to forgive.

You encountered all this through the narrative of a fictional character who met Jesus.

What is your story? Have you truly encountered Jesus?

If not, ask yourself, "Why not Jesus?"

If yes, it's time to ask others the question, "Why not Jesus?"

As you wrap up this study, use the following questions to spur on your personal growth in your relationship with Christ.

- How will you continue to seek God's kingdom first in your life?

- How will you make compassion a regular part of your Christian walk?

- How will you continue taking up your cross daily and following Jesus—even in His suffering?

- How will you help others come to know the message of hope and salvation you have found in Jesus Christ?

Conclude your time today in prayer, thanking God for this experience and asking Him for opportunities to live out your faith and call others to Him. His suffering was real. His forgiveness is real. Your encounter with Jesus matters. Helping others see Him might matter even more.

END NOTES

SESSION 1

[1] Thayer and Smith. "Greek Lexicon entry for Martus," *The NAS New Testament Greek Lexicon* [online] 1999 (cited 15 June 2016). Available from the Internet: www.biblestudytools.com.

[2] M.G. Easton M.A., *D.D. Illustrated Bible Dictionary, Third Edition,* published by Thomas Nelson [online] 1897 (cited 15 June 2016). Available from the Internet: www.biblestudytools.com.

[3] Thayer and Smith. "Greek Lexicon entry for Tekton," *The NAS New Testament Greek Lexicon* [online] 1999 (cited 15 June 2016). Available from the Internet: www.biblestudytools.com.

[4] "Was Jesus a Carpenter?" Eternity Bible College's Faculty Blog, accessed June 17, 2016, http://facultyblog.eternitybiblecollege.com/2011/12/was-jesus-a-carpenter/#.V19-J2YWE1i.

[5] John MacArthur, Twelve Ordinary Men (Nashville, TN: Thomas Nelson, 2002), 99.

SESSION 2

[1] Walter A. Elwell. "Entry for Compassion," *Baker's Evangelical Dictionary of Biblical Theology* [online] 1997 (cited 17 June 2016). Available from the Internet: www.biblestudytools.com.

[2] Thayer and Smith. "Greek Lexicon entry for Splagchnizomai," *The NAS New Testament Greek Lexicon* [online] 1999 (cited 17 June 2016). Available from the Internet: www.biblestudytools.com.

[3] "Caring for Widows," Grace to You, accessed June 17, 2016, http://www.gty.org/resources/study-guides/40-5209/caring-for-widows.

[4] Warren W. Wiersbe, *The Wiersbe Bible Commentary: The Complete New Testament in One Volume* (Colorado Springs, CO: David C. Cook, 2003), 34.

SESSION 3

[1] "The Risen Christ: Satisfied with His Suffering," DesiringGod.org, http://www.desiringgod.org/messages/the-risen-christ-satisfied-with-his-suffering (accessed 19 June 2016)

SESSION 4

[1] "D.T. Niles quotes," ThinkExist.com, accessed June 20, 2016, http://thinkexist.com/quotation/evangelism-is-just-one-beggar-telling-another/535387.html.

[2] Greg Laurie, *Tell Someone* (Nashville, TN: LifeWay, 2016), 20.

[3] "Mary Magdalene," *All Women of the Bible* [online] Zondervan 1988 (cited 19 June 2016). Available from the Internet: www.biblegateway.com.

[4] Greg Laurie, *Tell Someone* (Nashville, TN: LifeWay, 2016).

SESSION 5

[1] Thayer and Smith. "Greek Lexicon entry for Allelon," *The NAS New Testament Greek Lexicon* [online] 1999 (cited 18 June 2016). Available from the Internet: www.biblestudytools.com.

[2] Thayer and Smith. "Greek Lexicon entry for Eleos," *The NAS New Testament Greek Lexicon* [online] 1999 (cited 18 June 2016). Available from the Internet: www.biblestudytools.com.

[3] John MacArthur, *The MacArthur Bible Commentary* (Nashville, TN: Thomas Nelson, 2005), 1697.

[4] "Jesus' Authority to Forgive Sins," BibleGateway.com, accessed June 18, 2016, https://www.biblegateway.com/resources/commentaries/IVP-NT/Matt/Jesus-Authority-Forgive-Sins.

[5] Warren Wiersbe, *The Wiersbe Bible Commentary.* (Colorado Springs, CO: David C. Cook, 2007), 256.

NOTES

NOTES

NOTES

NOTES